Garfield

Gooooooal!

JiM DAViS

RAVETTE PUBLISHING

This edition first published by Ravette Publishing
in the Year 2000

Printed and bound in Great Britain
for Ravette Publishing Limited,
Unit 3, Tristar Centre,
Star Road, Partridge Green,
West Sussex RH13 8RA
by Cox & Wyman Ltd, Reading, Berkshire

ISBN: 1 84161 037 2

HAVE YOU HUGGED YOUR TREE TODAY?

I HAD A COMBING ACCIDENT THIS MORNING

© 1997 PAWS, INC./Distributed by Universal Press Syndicate

WERE THERE ANY SURVIVORS?

JIM DAVIS 4-30

© 1997 PAWS, INC./Distributed by Universal Press Syndicate

JIM DAVIS 5-7

JIM DAVIS 5-10

WE'RE BEING ANNOYING IN SHIFTS

© 1997 PAWS, INC./Distributed by Universal Press Syndicate

JIM DAVIS 5-23

© 1997 PAWS, INC./Distributed by Universal Press Syndicate

© 1997 PAWS, INC./Distributed by Universal Press Syndicate

© 1997 PAWS, INC./Distributed by Universal Press Syndicate

THE COFFEE TOOK
MY DONUT

COFFEE STRONG
ENOUGH
FOR YOU?

YEAH, BUT
THE DONUTS
ARE TOO
WEAK

BURP

© 1997 PAWS, INC./Distributed by Universal Press Syndicate

© 1997 PAWS, INC. /Distributed by Universal Press Syndicate

OTHER GARFIELD BOOKS AVAILABLE

Pocket Books	Price	ISBN
Bon Appetit	£3.50	1 84161 038 0
Byte Me	£2.99	1 84161 009 7
Double Trouble	£2.99	1 84161 008 9
A Gift For You	£3.50	1 85304 190 4
The Gladiator	£2.99	1 85304 941 7
Great Impressions	£2.99	1 85304 191 2
Hangs On	£2.99	1 85304 784 8
Here We Go Again	£2.99	0 948456 10 8
In The Pink	£2.99	0 948456 67 1
In Training	£2.99	1 85304 785 6
The Irresistible	£2.99	1 85304 940 9
Le Magnifique!	£3.50	1 85304 243 9
Let's Party	£2.99	1 85304 906 9
Light Of My Life	£3.50	1 85304 353 2
On The Right Track	£2.99	1 85304 907 7
On Top Of The World	£2.99	1 85304 104 1
Pick Of The Bunch	£2.99	1 85304 258 7
The Reluctant Romeo	£2.99	1 85304 391 5
Says It With Flowers	£2.99	1 85304 316 8
Shove At First Sight	£2.99	1 85304 990 5
Strikes Again	£2.99	0 906710 62 6
To Eat, Or Not To Eat?	£2.99	1 85304 991 3
Wave Rebel	£3.50	1 85304 317 6
With Love From Me To You	£2.99	1 85304 392 3

Theme Books @ £3.99 each	
Guide to Behaving Badly	1 85304 892 5
Guide to Being a Couch Potato	1 84161 039 9
Guide to Creatures Great and Small	1 85304 998 0
Guide to Friends	1 84161 040 2
Guide to Healthy Living	1 85304 972 7
Guide to Insults	1 85304 895 X
Guide to Pigging Out	1 85304 893 3
Guide to Romance	1 85304 894 1
Guide to The Seasons	1 85304 999 9
Guide to Successful Living	1 85304 973 5

Classics @ £4.99 each	**ISBN**
Volume One	1 85304 970 0
Volume Two	1 85304 971 9
Volume Three	1 85304 996 4
Volume Four	1 85304 997 2
Volume Five	1 84161 022 4
Volume Six	1 84161 023 2

Miscellaneous

Garfield Address Book	£4.99 inc. VAT	1 85304 904 2
Garfield 21st Birthday Celebration Book	£9.99	1 85304 995 6

All Garfield books are available at your local bookshop or from the address below. Just tick the titles required and send the form with your payment to:-

BBCS, P O Box 941, Kingston upon Hull HU1 3YQ
24-hour telephone credit card line 01482 224626
Prices and availability are subject to change without notice.
Please enclose a cheque or postal order made payable to BBCS to the value of the cover price of the book and allow the following for postage and packing:

UK & BFPO:	£1.95 (weight up to 1kg)	3-day delivery
	£2.95 (weight over 1kg up to 20kg)	3-day delivery
	£4.95 (weight up to 20kg)	next day delivery

EU & Eire:	Surface Mail	£2.50 for first book & £1.50 for subsequent books
	Airmail	£4.00 for first book & £2.50 for subsequent books
USA:	Surface Mail	£4.50 for first book & £2.50 for subsequent books
	Airmail	£7.50 for first book & £3.50 for subsequent books
Rest of	Surface Mail	£6.00 for first book & £3.50 for subsequent books
the World:	Airmail	£10.00 for first book & £4.50 for subsequent books

Name ....

Address ....

....

....

Cards accepted: Visa, Mastercard, Switch, Delta, American Express

Expiry Date.......................Signature ....